Around
Barrow-in-Furness
IN OLD PHOTOGRAPHS

Around Barrow-in-Furness

IN OLD PHOTOGRAPHS

Collected by JOHN GARBUTT
and JOHN MARSH

First published in 1993 by
Alan Sutton Publishing, an imprint of
Sutton Publishing Limited
Phoenix Mill · Thrupp · Stroud
Gloucestershire · GL5 2BU

Reprinted 1997

This book is dedicated to Diane and Gary
Curwen, who had a special launch in 1993

**British Library Cataloguing in
Publication Data**

Garbutt, John
 Barrow-in-Furness in Old Photographs
 I. Title II. Marsh, John
 942.781

ISBN 0 7509 0522 0

Typeset in 9/10 Sabon.
Typesetting and origination by
Sutton Publishing Limited.
Printed in Great Britain by
WBC Limited, Bridgend.

Contents

The medieval Piel Castle at the entrance to Barrow harbour.

Introduction

To those who live there the Barrow-in-Furness district is a quiet corner of north-west England filled with small villages of character, coastline on three sides for boating and fishing, open untouched countryside, easy access to the Lake District National Park, an equable climate, wind for kite flying, abundant wildlife, industrial archaeology in profusion, limited but easily accessible entertainments, good golf courses, and houses at lower prices than in the south. Furness stands guard over Morecambe Bay, an area outstanding for its birdlife, which is fed by the rivers Crake, Leven and Kent.

This book of old photographs depicting the Barrow area south of Ulverston is intended to complement its companion volume on *Lancashire North of the Sands*, also published by Alan Sutton. The two books take a nostalgic look at the area as it was about the turn of the century.

The authors are indebted to the historians of Furness such as R.S. Geddes, W. McGowan Gradon, J.L. Hobbs, Dr John D. Marshall, James Melville, James Park, Dr W. Rollinson, J. Richardson, Prof. Michael Twyman, James E. Walton, Thomas West and others, and to the early photographers, in particular for the Atkinson and Sankey series of postcards. They are to be envied for the hours they have spent engrossed in the rich heritage of this Furness area.

The early history of the area is to be found in the sand dunes of Walney Island and in the many prehistoric remains which dot the surrounding countryside. The Romans undoubtedly knew Furness for its iron and, possibly, the port of Barrow, but scholars are still seeking evidence of their presence here. The post-Roman history is related to the great Earldom of Northumbria and the Kingdom of Strathclyde, but archaeological evidence is again slight. The early Christians knew the place, and it was their church sites that were expanded in Norman times into the parishes we know today.

During the early medieval period the Barony of Kendal acquired much land from the Crown, as did the religious houses of the Cistercians at Furness and the Augustinians at Conishead, but throughout this time the site of the modern town of Barrow was but a few fishermen's huts on the seashores of Walney Channel. The most substantial building in the Barrow district then was the large wool warehouse on the Island of Fouldrey (the Piel of Fouldrey or Piel Castle).

The Reformation wrought great changes. By all accounts Furness was devastated by the loss of the great Cistercian Abbey of Furness and the infrastructure it made possible. Recovery was slow, centred on the two market towns of Dalton and Ulverston. It was in the latter that a great Nonconformist rebellion took place when George Fox called on the Fell family and together they founded the Society of Friends, which soon had an international following.

The first major change in the Barrow area for many thousands of years was the quest for iron in the eighteenth century. Together with the extensive woodlands and the technologies devised by the Industrial Revolution, this search led to the 'Early Iron Industry of Furness' described by Alfred Fell in 1908 in his book of that name.

The expansion of the iron industry and the realization that here was a superb, sheltered port led to the foundation of modern Barrow-in-Furness. Four men in particular were instrumental in the development of Barrow and district: Henry William Schneider, Sir James Ramsden, the Earl of Burlington (later the Duke of Devonshire), and the Duke of Buccleuch. Schneider, a London businessman of German descent, developed the rich Park iron mine. Ramsden is best known for the development of the Furness Railway, which included the Barrow docks. The Dukes of Devonshire and Buccleuch were the principle landowners and, with Schneider, the financiers. All were involved in the Barrow steelworks.

This book takes readers back to those days at the turn of this century when Barrow, its port, steelworks and shipyard were in their heyday. The town of Dalton and the surrounding villages of Low Furness shared the prosperity of the time. The photographs also touch on what has been termed 'the long decline', with the depression years of the 1920s and '30s leading to the Second World War. Transport in those days was for the most part by the Furness Railway and horse carriage, but also to be seen are the sea trips which could be had to Ireland, the Isle of Man and across Morecambe Bay to Fleetwood.

Triumphs, tragedies and humour will all be found in this miscellany of photographs of an area unique in the British Isles.

J. Garbutt
J. Marsh
Summer 1993

SECTION ONE

Sea, Sand and Ferries

All aboard for the trip to the Isle of Man on 4 August 1924. This was a special trip for the annual combined August holiday and Vickers (Barrow) holiday week, although before Heysham harbour was built in 1904 a regular Isle of Man service was run from Barrow.

On board the SS *Robina* from Fleetwood for Barrow on 5 September 1922, by which time the end of the Fleetwood to Barrow trip was nearly in sight. The *Robina* was run by the New Morecambe Central Pier Company on a route which the Furness Railway tried to make their own before the First World War. The LMS Railway, having Heysham as a port, virtually abandoned Barrow.

The SS *Philomel* (or 'full of smell' – see p. 17) was on the Fleetwood run from Barrow for seven years. Here Sankeys of Barrow pictured the mainly male passengers on the 18 September 1909 outward trip from Barrow. Note the background of funnel smoke.

On board the *Lady Evelyn* (see p. 16) outward bound to Fleetwood on 18 June 1910. The cruising was advertised 'every weekday from June 1st to September 30th'. The return trip to the Lakes 'round fare', including Furness Abbey, Windermere Lake and Coniston, was 1st class and saloon 11s. 6d., 3rd class and cabin 7s. 6d. from Blackpool or 10s. and 6s. 9d. from Fleetwood. The *Lady Evelyn* cruised at 14 knots and took about one and a quarter hours to cross the bay with a maximum 715 passengers.

Passengers on board the *Gwalia* on a trip to Fleetwood on 16 May 1910. The Furness Railway had recently acquired the new ship, which was renamed the *Lady Moyra* soon after its arrival.

The newly named *Lady Moyra* outward bound to Fleetwood and Blackpool on 18 August 1913. With accommodation for 1,014 passengers and a speed of 19 knots the *Lady Moyra* could cross the bay 'in about an hour'.

The *Gwalia* approaching Fleetwood in 1910. Built originally for the Barry Railway Company she was the Furness Railway's largest steamer. Mrs Parsons, the stewardess, looked to the passengers' needs, especially the seasick, and entertainment was provided by a harpist, a violinist and a cornet player, who were rewarded 'when the indispensible bag was passed round'. Edward Sankey, or the 'camera fiend', as he was called, was very busy on these trips, taking, and then processing, pictures in both directions, so that the southbound Barrow crowds on the early morning trip, as well as the northbound Blackpool and Fleetwood crowds, could purchase postcards on their return journey. It is recorded that in the 1911 season Sankey took 2,000 negatives on the boats and 'sold tens of thousands of these interesting souvenirs, some passengers being taken more oftener than they cared'.

The magnificent paddle-steamer, the *Lady Moyra*. During the 1911 season Captain Ashcroft, who had worked the route from its beginning some ten years before, took over the *Lady Moyra* with first mate, John Helm and second mate, Mr E. Vardon. The chief engineer was Mr F. Hewitt and the second engineer, Mr E. Kelsall, both Furness Railway trained men. The purser was Mr Henry Brown. It was reported that in the 1911 season, 'which was the first that the boats had not to lie up through heavy weather, 189,936 passengers were conveyed to and fro in the company's delightful steamers, the *Lady Moyra* and the *Lady Evelyn*'. It is a pity this holiday facility is now rarely available on the Barrow coast. (Photo by Raphael Tuck for the Furness Railway.)

The same boat in the 1930s, renamed the *Brighton Queen* after being acquired by Campbells. The boat became part of Campbells' south coast fleet, making journeys along the south coast and across to continental ports. The *Brighton Queen* was sunk while taking part in the rescue of the British Expeditionary Force from the beaches at Dunkirk in 1940.

The *Lady Evelyn* ploughing her way across Morecambe Bay before the First World War. She was built in 1900 by Scotts on the Clyde and was the first ship to start the Barrow to Fleetwood service for the Furness Railway under Captain Williams, who was the first skipper on the route. Captain Thomas and Captain Quinn were later skippers before Captain Hill took over about the time the photograph was taken. Captain Hill had been senior tugmaster for the Furness Railway for many years and had served the company for a total of twenty-one years when he became captain of the *Lady Evelyn*, with Mr W. Harrison as the chief engineer and Mr G. McDowall as second engineer. Mr J. Hunt was the first mate and Mr J. Iddon second mate, with Miss Doran as stewardess and Mr J. Newton as purser. The *Lady Evelyn* was also acquired by Campbells after the First World War, and renamed the *Brighton Belle*. She too was lost at Dunkirk in 1940.

The *Philomel*, a smokey paddle-steamer which local wags renamed the 'full of smell'. During her career with the Furness Railway from 1903 to 1910 she worked on the Barrow to Fleetwood and Blackpool crossings. She was bought to assist the *Lady Evelyn* and was replaced by the *Lady Moyra*. Another ship, the *Lady Margaret*, was also used for a short time on this route. The route was started with the aim of bringing Blackpool visitors 'on an agreeable diversification to journey down to Fleetwood by tram or electric car and board a Furness Railway steamer, imbibing the invigorating ozone from the sea and proceed by rail, gondola and coach right into the heart of the English Lakeland. Surely an agreeable change from the human maelstrom of Blackpool, or the ceaseless turmoil of the city.'

Fishers of Newry's SS *Oak* and the North Lonsdale Iron and Steel Company's *City of Liverpool* from Ulverston unloading ballast in the hope of floating off into the channel on the next tide. The sands surrounding the approach to Barrow Harbour were difficult to negotiate even for local captains.

The twin funnel Barrow tugboat *Furness* and four prawner yachts, on a postcard dated 1906. On the back of the card Ethel writes 'Please excuse the picture it's the only one I've got.'

Prawner yachts on a postcard from the 1920s entitled 'Walney Island from the Ferry'. These fine clinker-built boats, many constructed at Arnside by Crossfields, lasted many years around the Morecambe Bay and some are still in use today.

The Walney Ferry, the Ferry Hotel and, in the background, the Barrow Steelworks (see p. 22) at the turn of the century before the age of the motor car.

Large crowds on board the Walney Ferry, which at one time travelled over the channel. This, the last of the ferry boats, ceased to run when the bridge between Barrow Island and Walney was opened in 1908, and there is a rumour that the hulk of this boat is rusting away near Southampton. Both pictures date to the turn of the century.

The chain-propelled ferry on a quieter day in the early twentieth century. The steam ferry was built in 1878 at Barrow Shipyard for the Furness Railway Company. Originally, two fords across the channel had been dredged away to improve the harbour but the steam ferry still had to be supported by row-boat ferries as the population of Walney increased. The ferry was nick-named 'the Vickerstown torturer' and the inhabitants of Walney asked why they were marooned between 12 midnight and 5.30 a.m. when the ferry boat did not run.

The extensive iron and steelworks shown from across the Walney Channel at the turn of the century. Iron and steelworks at Millom, Askam, Barrow and Ulverston lit up the night sky of the local coastline for many years and became part of the 'sights' of the area. All have now gone.

Yachting in Walney Channel on a full tide. The Royal Barrow Yacht Club had the Earl of Dalkeith as its commodore and Sir James Ramsden as its vice-commodore in the late nineteenth century.

Vickerstown across the channel, *c.* 1902. The claim that Vickerstown was a 'marine garden city' was enhanced by views such as this.

Seeking fresh air at Walney in the early days of the century. Using an umbrella as a parasol to safeguard a pale complexion, maybe these visitors were wiser than our generation in their approach to the sun, but how did they cope with the formal dress for all outings?

Tanks and field guns at Walney in the 1920s. After the First World War these appeared as a memento of the war to end all wars. The ladies present no doubt hoped that it was, as many were widowed or remained spinsters as a result of the conflict.

Summer crowds at Biggar Bank. Not many industrial towns such as Barrow could boast 'holiday' facilities for its workers. A few pence fare on the ferry, or later the Biggar Bank tram, provided all the sea and sand a family could possibly require. The weather, as ever, could be a problem.

A Whit Monday crowd at Biggar Bank, *c.* 1907. The postcard carries the message 'having a quiet time with sloppy ice cream'. In the background a pierrot entertains the crowd from a stage.

Roa Island from the sea shows a much changed scene from today. A full tide laps at the base of the ramp to the old lifeboat station. In 1852 the Furness Railway bought Roa Island from John Abel Smith, who had bought the island in 1840 with a view to running a ferry service across Morecambe Bay. On the right, with its tower, is Schneider Cottage, built in 1860 for Henry Schneider, mine owner and director of the iron and steelworks.

Piel Castle, *c.* 1905. Said to have been built as a fortified wool warehouse by the Cistercian monks of Furness Abbey, the Piel of Fouldrey, to use its ancient name, is still an impressive guardian of the entrance to the modern harbour of Barrow.

The Furness Railway station and Roa Island Hotel, *c.* 1905. This was the original port of Barrow, where a pier was built in 1846 and a railway station in 1847. Piel Pier became disused when Ramsden Dock was opened in 1879 and was finally removed in 1891, parts going to make a pier at Grange-over-Sands. The station continued in use until 1936. Thomas Pennington was the landlord at the hotel at the time of the photograph.

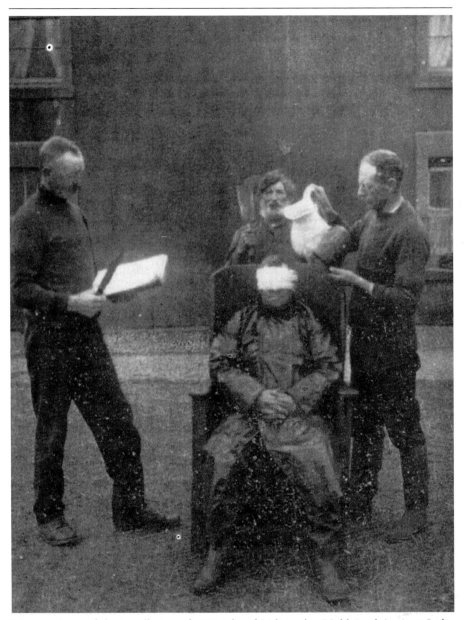

The ceremony of the installation of a 'Knight of Piel' to the 'Noble and Ancient Order of the Knights of Piel', *c.* 1919. The King of Piel (or the landlord of the Ship Inn) stands with knife and charter while an assistant pours a gallon of beer over the new knight, who is blindfolded and dressed in oilskins and wellingtons. The new knight's duty was then to buy a round of drinks, after which he gained the right of a free night's lodging if he was ever shipwrecked on Piel. With many knights also being fishermen, this was not as far-fetched as it might at first sound!

The coast road in the late 1930s. Built in the 1920s and '30s, the road was constructed partly to give work to the unemployed, and is seen here with an open tourer car, registration no. KU 7336. Until well after the Second World War, this was the best rural road in Furness. Some of the hard core for the new road came from the demolition of the Dunn family's Stank mine buildings (see pp. 134 and 135).

The coast road at the Point of Comfort at Goadsbarrow Bay in the 1930s. Local bus companies ferried Furness and Barrow families along the coast road to one of the popular beaches, many a family man dreaming of owning a car such as an Austin 7 to take his wife and children without having to wait for the bus.

Vickers Platers on a day trip along the coast road to Bardsea in 1910. J.G. informs Miss M. Jackson at the Girls' Friendly Society Home of Rest at Bare, Morecambe, that the photograph was 'taken just behind the Mill', and asks 'Do you think you can pick me out on it as I will have altered a little since you saw me last.'

Summer holiday crowds on the Duddon Estuary shore on the north coast of Furness at Askam, c. 1910. Posted in 1914 at the outbreak of the First World War, the postcard rather ominously reads, 'We hear that Will's got his papers.'

SECTION TWO

Docks, Shipyard and Industry

PORT OF BARROW

An informative engraving of the SS *City of Rome* passing through the 100 ft wide entrance to Ramsden Dock. The engraving featured in the large illustrated guide, *The Furness Railway Company's Docks. Port of Barrow*, published by the Furness Railway Co. in 1895. On the right hand quayside are trains of horse-drawn railway coal tubs.

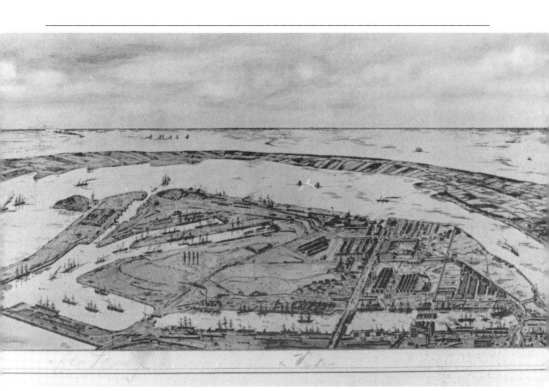

There is hardly a steamship in site in this bird's-eye view of Barrow Docks, which is included in the Barrow-in-Furness illustrated Almanack and Tide Table of 1887. *Mannex's Guide and Directory of Furness*, 1882, says, 'The formal opening of the docks took place on the 19th of September 1867 admist rejoicings and festivities. Among the speakers at the banquet was the Rt. Hon. W.E. Gladstone.' Ramsden Dock was completed in 1879.

Two small cantilever cranes load a steamer on the busy Anchor Line wharves in a branch of Ramsden Dock. Mannex's guide, *c.* 1895, says 'In 1879, the Anchor Line company commenced running one of their splendid steamers between Barrow and New York every alternate Wednesday.' Note the mistrust of steam in the ample for'ard mast with sails.

The SS *City of Rome*, launched in 1881, in Barrow Dock entrance basin during her fitting-out period. Mannex records in 1882, 'The company's chef d'oeuvre is the magnificent screw steamer *The City of Rome* launched on the 14th June 1881. This is the largest vessel ever built, next to the *Great Eastern*. Her entire length is 550 feet, tonnage 8,333, and horse power 1,500. This magnificent piece of naval architecture is a triumph of which the company may be proud.'

The foreign animal wharves and chill rooms near the dock's entrance basin, *c.* 1895. In the foreground is the grain warehouse and behind the sheds are the cattle lairs sufficient for a thousand head. In the distance are the slaughterhouses for cattle and pigs.

The interior of the slaughterhouse, *c.* 1895. Mannex reports that they had 'every other convenience for the supply of distant markets with fresh meat', and goes on, 'this abbatoir has been mentioned by the highest authority in the land as a model which other ports might usefully imitate.'

The PS *Duchess of Buccleuch* taking on passengers at Ramsden Dock station, Barrow, *c.* 1900. Note the two level landing stage on the left.

The 'floating and depositing dock' – a precursor to the dry dock. It was built for the Barrow Docks and Railway Company and for a time was unique in Britain. Here seen in Devonshire Dock, *c.* 1895, it could raise and deposit a 3,200 ton vessel on to an outrigger pontoon. Its use was fully described in Mannex 1882, which says 'a similar dock constructed by the same firm for the Russian government is now in operation in the Black Sea.'

Barrow shipbuilding works in the 1890s. Two ships are berthed, one being fitted from the 100 ton crane on the depositing dockside. What a difference from the scene in Devonshire Dock today.

No. 6 of the C class of submarines moored in the Walney Channel. Built at Barrow in 1906, it was one of forty-two submarines launched at Barrow between 1905 and 1910. Reportedly less than seaworthy, it was succeeded by the bigger and faster D class in 1907. C6 was scrapped in 1919.

The Furness Railway diver with his attendant on their boat early this century. (Photo by W. Ralph of No. 51 Glasgow Street, Barrow.)

J. Thompson of No. 54 Blake Street, Barrow, put together this postcard of the 1911 airship wreck. On the reverse, Emily wrote to Susie, 'How do you like our new airship – isn't it a reck. I went down to see it a week last Sunday, the day it came out and there were thousands of people.'

The airship *Mayfly* in 1911. It was first launched at 4 a.m. on Monday 22 May but was taken back into the assembly shed after four days for modification. The upper photograph depicts the spectacular result of the attempt to launch the airship on 24 September. After the incident, the wreck was dismantled with a loss estimated at £70,000. The lower picture shows the huge airship shed under construction, *c.* 1910.

HMS *Vanguard* sails out to sea through Buccleuch Bridge via Ramsden Dock in 1910. This Dreadnought class battleship became famous in 1917 when she exploded at anchor in Scapa Flow killing over eight hundred of her crew.

The launch of HMS *Powerful* from what was then called the 'Barrow launching ground' on 24 July 1895. This was the first cruiser built at Barrow and the largest afloat at the time. The boat proved to be too cumbersome and she ended her days as a depot ship.

Laying the keel of the 9,750 ton cruiser HMS *Cumberland* on 18 October 1924. A cruiser of the Kent class (HMS *Kent* was launched on the same day at Chatham), the *Cumberland* was launched on 16 March 1926 by the Dowager Countess of Carlisle, who had launched the previous HMS *Cumberland* on the Clyde in 1902. The first commanding officer was Captain A.L. Snagge RN. After a distinguished career the ship was scrapped in 1959. The lower picture shows the ship being fitted out.

A familiar shape on the Barrow skyline, the 150 ton Vickers wharf crane towers over the warships being fitted out in Devonshire Dock.

The high level bridge between Barrow and Barrow Island, open to allow the passage of a small steamer out of Devonshire Dock, about the turn of the century.

An aerial view of the entrance to Ramsden Dock shows the busy Anchor Line sheds on the left with rail links to the dock and main lines. The scene is much changed today.

Five large boats being constructed on the six slipways at the Messrs Vickers Limited Naval Construction Works. Will this scene ever be repeated?

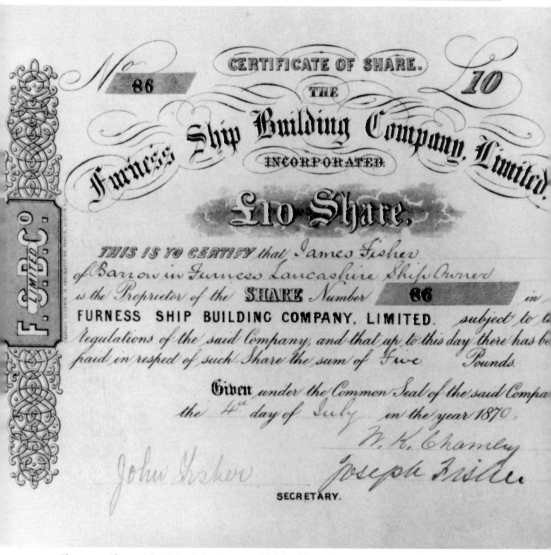

Share certificate No. 86 of the Furness Shipbuilding Company Limited, issued in 1870 to James Fisher. The first sod of the construction of the shipbuilding works was cut in December of the same year. James Fisher's company, ship owners and shipping agents, had its office at No. 29 The Strand and the new shipbuilding company at No. 32 The Strand. It is worth noting that John Fisher signed the certificate as company secretary and Joseph Fisher as a director.

Three warships, HMSs *Doris*, *Powerful* and *Juno*, with the 100 ton crane at Devonshire fitting-out dock in early 1896.

Engineers experiment with models in Devonshire Dock in 1896. A shipyard report accompanying the photograph said, 'in connection with the design of torpedo boat destroyers. The model is towed at the lower end of a long balanced lever, the connection being a wire link hooked to the lever, and to a bulkhead left in the model when hollowed out.'

The Japanese battleship *Katori*, which was being fitted out, and some of her crew (Togo's Tars), trained by Vickers Sons & Maxim Ltd at Barrow in 1906.

A two-funnelled paddle-wheeled tug nudges the starboard side of the battleship *Katori* on 28 May 1906. The postcard was sent from Portsmouth by crew member A. Ishikawa to B. Sandham Esq. of No. 4 Stewart Street, Barrow, on 5 June 1906. He says, 'We have to leave good old England on the 9th and I want to say Goodbye. May you have all prosperity and happiness in your future.'

Mr Winston Churchill's two-day visit to Barrow commencing 25 September 1912 was part of 'The most comprehensive tour of private firms engaged in naval construction ever undertaken by any First Sea Lord.' The top picture shows the Admiralty steam yacht *Enchantress*, on board which Churchill arrived from the Clyde, and the lower picture shows his arrival at Ramsden Dock complete with familiar cigar and bowler.

Mr Churchill inspecting the Vickers engine works, with Sir Trevor Dawson, Mr James McKechnie and Mr Archibald Miller, directors of the Vickers company, in 1912. A newspaper report of the time stated 'Mr Churchill will no doubt return to Whitehall with a fuller knowledge as to the problems associated with the provision of material to maintain British supremacy than can have been the case with many of his predecessors.'

Hugh Rainey & Co.'s 'turnout' for the Barrow hospital parade on 11 September 1909. The cart was decorated by Vickers Sons & Maxim ordnance department, who provided Chinese lanterns and a 'Whitehead' torpedo. Messrs Rainey were farmers and carting contractors of North Scale, Walney.

Devonshire Dock warehouses and Walmsley and Smith's corn mill, which appeared in
The Furness Railway Company's Docks. Port of Barrow in 1895. The signal-box carries
the notice 'Cornmill crossing'.

Frame binding slabs at Vickers Sons & Maxim Ltd (see front cover). Vickers' problems
in modernizing marine construction are shown in their 1896 guide, which reports that
'the use of hydraulic rivetters had been discarded owing to the popularity of channel
and Z-sections . . . the preference for which was early recognised at Barrow but the
large amount of Admiralty work now entrusted has induced the management to resume
hydraulic rivetting.'

Electric drillers at work on HMS *Niobe* in 1896. Vickers reported, 'The engine and dynamo were fitted on one bed-plate placed on the deck, steam being supplied from a portable donkey boiler.'

Part of the core-making and moulding department of Vickers Armstrongs Ltd. The picture originally appeared in their trade brochure *Iron and Steel Castings* in the 1920s.

The largest of eight plate edge planing machines in the Vickers works in 1896. 'This splendid tool is capable of planing simultaneously the butt and seam edges of plates 30 foot in length and 7 foot in width,' said the shipyard report.

Vickers Armstrongs castings were advertised in the 1920s by such photographs as this. 'The value of Perlit iron in the manufacture of casting where heat resisting qualities combined with strength are necessary, is of great importance,' stated Vickers *Iron and Steel Castings* brochure.

Inside the pattern shop of Vickers Armstrongs Ltd, 'which, being fitted with the most up-to-date woodworking machines, enables us to manufacture patterns on competitively economical lines . . . and to give service equal to any other pattern shop in the British Isles,' said Vickers 1920s brochure.

The test house at Vickers Armstrongs Ltd, where they advertised 'the chief chemist is in control, where mechanical testing of all classes of material is carried out, and records of all metals tested are carefully kept. The chains in the foreground are used for lifting and drawing in our shops.'

Stern frame castings, weighing 22 tons and measuring 40 ft, being assembled in Vickers Armstrongs works in the 1920s.

A stern frame mould being produced in one of the large moulding pits at the foundry of Vickers Armstrongs Ltd in the 1920s. 'By being able to mould and cast work of this class on these lines the feeding methods can be attended to in a manner which ensures the best possible conditions for production,' said the 1920s castings brochure.

The Bessemer furnace at Barrow Steelworks. Schneider, Hanney and Co. erected the blast furnaces at Hindpool in 1859. After the transfer to the Barrow Haematite Iron & Steel Co. in 1864 'the operation of converting iron into steel by the recently perfected process of Mr Bessemer was carried on,' said Mannex's guide.

The steel plate mill at Barrow Steelworks in 1899. Mannex's guide of 1882 stated 'the steel company have 14 eight ton converters, 3 rail mills with hydraulic lifts, 1 plate mill, 2 merchant mills and 2 tyre mills.'

SECTION THREE
Life in Barrow

The town centre showing the back of the Town Hall, on a busy market-day in the 1920s. The covered market, built by Paley of Lancaster in 1866, is behind the Town Hall and the 'open' market can be seen with crowds in the street.

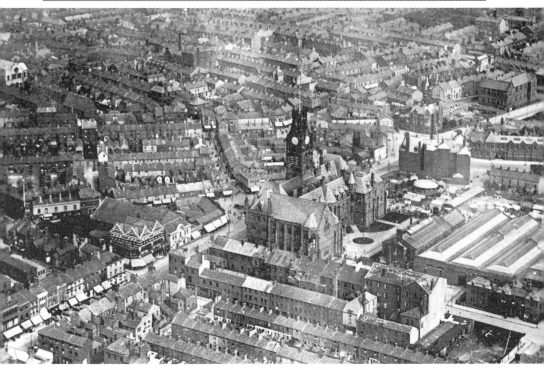

The Town Hall from the Ramsden Square side. The Town Hall, which dominates this area, was opened by the Marquis of Hartington in 1887 in a great celebration (see p. 99). The architect was W.H. Lynn of Belfast. Pevsner says, 'Large, a monument to Barrow's prosperity.' This is a much changed scene today.

The Schneider Square area. The top view shows the traffic-free 'square' with the Albion Hotel on the corner, *c.* 1902. The statue to Henry William Schneider was unveiled in 1891 by the then Mayor of Barrow, Augustus Horace Strongitharm, mining engineer of Priors Lea. Schneider was Barrow's third mayor, and held office for three years from 1875. The statue shows him in mayoral robes. Note the iron railings. In the lower picture, taken about the time of the First World War, the double tram lines can be seen in front of the Town Hall, where the Cavendish statue contemplates the scene.

The view towards the Town Hall from Ramsden Square. In the top picture the statue of James Ramsden can be seen with its railings and lamp-posts, as originally installed. James Ramsden was Barrow's first mayor, holding office for five years from 1867. His statue, built by public subscription at a cost of £2,944, was unveiled on Whit Tuesday 1872 by the Duke of Devonshire 'amid great rejoicing and festivity'. The tram in the background has a panel advertising E. Todd and Sons, tailors, of No. 197 Dalton Road. In the lower picture the double-decker tram in Duke Street advertises Nestlé's Milk.

This is a typical 'novelty' postcard from before the First World War. The novelty was an opening flap, which contained a series of photographs of the town on a strip of paper. Posted in Barrow on 26 August 1914 at ½d. postage, it also carries a postage due stamp for 1d. as this type of postcard was 'liable for the letter rate'. However, the words 'no charge' are pencilled in, which must have pleased Miss Bertha Allen of Leeds, who was being asked by Eveline 'don't you wish you were coming in the auto to Barrow, how is your face keeping, please excuse writing, bit of a rush'.

Alice Woodburn and her sister, Florrie. Alice, the caretaker's daughter, died in a blaze at the Barrow Amateur Cycling and Athletic Club building on 17 February 1907. The building was housed in the old Royal Hotel and had been opened in 1902. The fire occurred during a gale, and damage was caused to the value of £1,500 (a considerable sum of money in those days). Although four-year-old Alice sadly perished, a report of the event added that there had been 'many exciting escapes'. The postcard was printed after the fire, sales receipts going to the family's benefit.

Exterior and interior views of the Furness Railway's central station at Barrow before the Second World War bombs altered its appearance. In the top view the glass case for *Coppernob* (see p. 72) is on the right and the wide approach from Abbey Road can be clearly seen. In the lower view from the 1920s the interior is a busy scene with passengers waiting for both north- and southbound trains.

A southbound train at Barrow station about the time of the First World War. A K.4 class 4–4–0 engine is assisted by a K.2 4–4–0. The brilliance of Sankey's photography of industrial and transport scenes is matched here by the condition of the two locomotives, showing pride in both studio and engine shed.

No. 3 0–4–0 *Coppernob*, a very famous engine from the early days of the Furness Railway. Seen in the top picture at the turn of the century, the engine was in service from 1846 to 1899. The view below, *c*. 1910, shows the engine in its glass show-case in front of the central station. The engine was damaged by bombing in the Second World War and is now in York Railway Museum, the bomb damage still apparent.

Furness Railway stock from the turn of the century. The engine shown above is a 2–2–2 tank engine No. 35, past stock which ran from 1866 to 1896, and below is a 'new train', drawn by K.2 4–4–0 No. 34. (Both photos are by Raphael Tuck for the Furness Railway postcard series.)

Mayor Robert Bateson Dixon Bradshaw leaves church on Mayoral Sunday, 17 November 1912. Alderman Bradshaw, a solicitor who lived at Risedale and had an office at No. 7 Lawson Street, sent the picture to a friend and wrote on the back of the postcard, 'I am in a hurry to get away from the church – we had 50 minutes of a sermon.' Mr Bradshaw was the alderman for Newbarns Ward and represented the Council on the Lancashire County Rating Committee and on the Billincoat Charity Trust.

Two important visitors to Barrow. In the top photograph the Duke of Kent is pictured in Ramsden Square on 19 October 1936 when he visited the 'social and occupational centres established for the benefit of the unemployed'. Staying with the Stanley family at Witherslack Hall, the duke can be seen here visiting the 'Voluntary Occupational Centre' in Ramsden Square. 'Look after your children,' said the duke to one unemployed man, 'things will alter.' In 1939 they undoubtedly did. In the lower scene Lord Frederick James Woolton briefs local press men in a wartime visit in June 1941. The former maths teacher and one-time merchandizing director for Lewis's Store, Manchester, was originally from Liverpool and became Minister of Supply in 1939 and Minister of Food in 1940.

Two of Shirtliffe John Priest's customers pose stiffly in their best clothes for what may well have been a wedding photograph sometime in the 1880s. A busy photographer in Barrow in the late nineteenth and early twentieth centuries, Priest had his photographic studios at No. 22 Paxton Terrace and No. 2 Thomas Street.

I had some difficulty
finding *my* apartments at
Barrow

A postcard by Cynicus of Tayport, *c.* 1905, illustrating the migration of workers from elsewhere to Barrow. Cynicus had much to say about Edwardian life, but really missed the time of great expansion, which is said to have ended in the early 1880s. Vickers continued to draw many from afar and even used an old liner as accommodation.

Barrow Public Park. The top picture dates from the late 1920s and shows families enjoying the park, which was built over a period of years on land acquired in 1901. The 'rough and uneven ground', as described in a 1907 directory, is still obvious in the lower photograph, taken some years later.

Barrow Public Park. The top photograph shows crowds enjoying the park just before the First World War. In the lower picture the 'inaugural trip' of a motor launch on the park lake in the 1920s is recorded.

A family party in front of the bandstand in Barrow Park, *c.* 1910. The bandstand was presented to the Borough by Alderman John Peter Smith JP of Arndene. The photograph was taken by Albert Turner, 'Photo Specialist', of No. 18 Robert Street, who also had a phonograph shop at No. 6 Crellin Street and was the insurance agent for the Royal London Insurance.

The fire-engine *Catherine E. Butler* with 'Merryweather's Hatfield pump' being tested in the streets round the Town Hall in 1911. The superintendent of the fire brigade run by the Borough Council was James H. Blezard. Alderman Butler was Mayor of Barrow at the time and the engine was named by and after his wife.

Burrell 7hp steam traction-engine No. 3562 *Lightning II*, registered number AO 6302, in Abbey Road, Barrow, on the way to take part in Barrow carnival in the early 1950s. The engine was bought by the travelling family fair Emerson and Hazard in 1913, to replace an earlier Fowler engine, also called *Lightning*. *Lightning II* continued in fairground use until just after the Second World War, when the fair acquired a replacement in the form of one of the huge ex-military diesel lorries that were being sold 'ex-WD' at the time. It was saved from scrap by Mr Bill Stables of Ulverston, who stored it on a piece of lane off Neville Street, Ulverston. It was taken on only a few excursions, Mr Stables complaining of the high road tax.

A Barrow ladies hockey team, about the time of the First World War. Players include C. Wilkins, M. Biggam, J. Brown, Olive Honeyman, E. Myers, A. Myers, D. Toothill and Miss Hewson.

The Barrow gas mask issue, due to 'the International Crisis' in 1938. The 'civilian anti-gas school' was at No. 80 Dalton Road, Barrow, with Police Sergeant Hughes in charge. There were two gas mask stores, one at No. 70 Hindpool Road, in the old jute mill offices, and one at No. 66 Abbey Road, in the Alexandra hut.

Sloop Street and Ship Street on wash-day at the turn of the century. This Barrow Island development from the 1880s copied Scottish industrial flats, when replacements for some wood shacks were ordered by the Duke of Devonshire and the Barrow Shipbuilding Company using a Dundee contractor.

Honeyman's shop on the corner of Ship Street. 'Butcher, Fruiterer and Shipping Supplier' is advertised. William George Honeyman, the owner, lived at Castle House, Gleaston. In the middle distance can be seen two ice-cream handcarts and three coal delivery horse-drawn carts.

Two former industrial buildings in Barrow. The top picture is of the Jute works at the turn of the century. The works was opened in 1872 by the Barrow Flax and Jute Company and exploited the female labour available in the town. The Jute works was 'a disastrous story' financially and the works also suffered two major fires. Below is the Barrow Steam Corn Mills (see p. 56) 'where Diamond O comes from, a modern mill using 1,000 tons weekly of the world's selected wheats'. The original enterprise was taken over by Walmsley and Smith in 1880 after it had 'suffered from management difficulty'. The corn mill picture was, remarkably, used as a greeting card in December 1907 to Mr Satterthwaite of Lane Head Greenodd to say 'Happy New Year – this is where Mr. works'. More details of these two industries can be found in Dr J.D. Marshall's *Furness and the Industrial Revolution*.

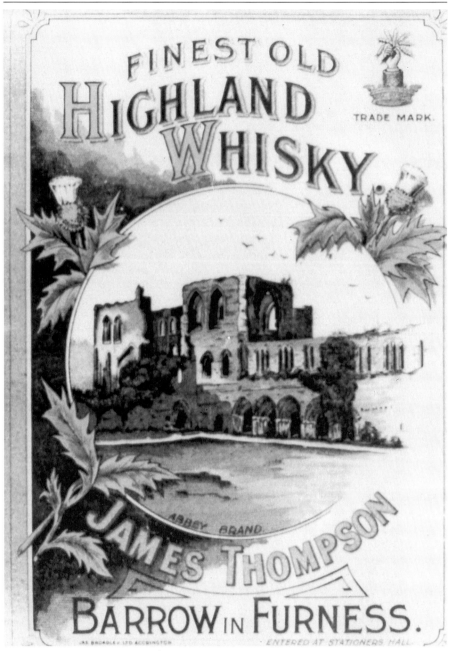

James Thompson & Co. Ltd, Wine and Spirit Merchants, of No. 237 Dalton Road, also had a mineral water factory in Dalkeith Street. Robert Thompson, the then owner, who lived at Ellerslie in Prospect Road, also traded in a 'finest old Highland Whisky' for those in town who considered his mineral water needed a little something extra.

Did this soldier survive the war? A recruit into the King's Own Regiment at the time of the First World War. The 4th Territorial Battn., The King's Own Regiment, was based at Ulverston and its C, D, E and F Companies had their drill hall on The Strand at Barrow. Note the goldfish in the sweet jar on the window-sill.

North Lonsdale Hospital, Barrow, *c*. 1905. The hospital owed its origins to the St George's hospital of 1866. Revd Barratt, the vicar of St George's, and a committee of ladies ran this hospital which, after expansion into School Street, was still found to be too small. The Furness Railway gave some land, Paley & Austin of Lancaster were hired as architects and a gloomy, institutional type of hospital was erected after many local donations had been collected. The top postcard has a message from Willie Graham, writing to his 'dear wife' at No. 76 Holker Street, informing her that he 'will be fit for home about Wednesday'. The lower picture shows the sister and nurses with patients on the men's ward.

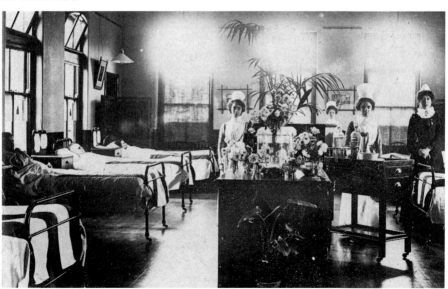

The children's ward at Christmas in the 1930s. The notice above the door reads 'fairyland'. Some of the patients might have thought otherwise.

Miss Marjorie Poles is crowned queen on the steps of the Town Hall during the annual charity fund-raising event for the hospital on 7 September 1935. (See also overleaf and pp. 118, 119.)

Crowds opposite the Town Hall for the parade on 19 September 1908. The message on the back of this postcard reads, 'The processions in the afternoon and evening were splendid. This picture shows the car representing the Snow Queen.' The parade that year enjoyed a fine day with crowded streets. The street collection came to £117.

A manly-looking group of 'lady cleaners' in their attempt to 'Clean up the Debt' for the Barrow Hospital parade of 22 September 1934. The cleaning brushes were designed to extract the pennies from the waiting crowds.

The opening of the Walney Bridge, 30 July 1908. In the top picture the crowds push forward to observe the horse carriage procession of the Mayor and Mayoress, Alderman and Mrs T.F. Butler of Infield, who opened the bridge, and in the lower view the troops assemble for the ceremony. Not many today will remember that the bridge was a toll-bridge from its opening until 1935 (the original toll was a halfpenny). The total cost of constructing the bridge was 'not less than £175,000'. In 1911 it was reported that 'about 50,000 people crossed the bridge every week', which would produce an income of nearly £105 per week from foot passengers alone.

The interior of St Paul's church, Barrow, *c.* 1905. Note the eagle lectern and the organ, which was presented by Councillor James Thompson of Monks' Croft. Following the setting up of St Paul's parish, Newbarns and Hawcoat were detached from Dalton to become part of the growing Borough of Barrow. In 1878 St George's (1860), St James's (1869) and St Paul's (1871) were joined by temporary brick-built churches dedicated to the evangelists Matthew, Mark, Luke and John. These were all dedicated on the same day (26 September) – 'an event so unique,' said a guide, 'records of past ages and annals of older towns will be searched in vain for a similar occurrence'.

St Paul's church, *c*. 1910. The polluting influence of motor transport, the side effects of which have surrounded the site for some decades, had not yet changed this road junction. The Strawberry Hotel, a busy garage and traffic dominate the scene today. After bomb damage in the Second World War St Paul's was repaired by Mawsons of Kendal.

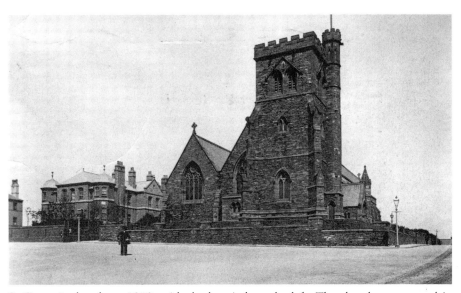

St George's church, *c*. 1910, with the hospital on the left. The church was erected in 1859–60 to designs by Paley of Lancaster as the parish church of Barrow. As the Borough grew, St George's became a parish in 1872 and then that parish was divided as other churches were built.

St James's church and school, as illustrated in a book by S. Jeavons of Paxton Terrace, at the turn of the century. Dedicated at Whit 1869, St James was a new church for an expanding town with a 'large and commodious school with accommodation for 800 children'.

Harvest Festival inside the Abbey Road Baptist chapel just after the First World War. This chapel was built in 1873 on land given by the Duke of Devonshire, the galleries being added in 1877, along with a schoolroom. All was to be destroyed in the German bombing of 1941 (see p. 121).

St Mary's Roman Catholic church (*c.* 1902) was built in Duke Street on land given by the Duke of Devonshire in 1866/7 to the design of E.W. Pugin, the son of the famous architect, A.W.N. Pugin. The writer of the Mannex guide of 1882 gives as much space to this church as almost all the other Barrow churches put together, even recording how the water-powered organ by Hill & Son, erected in 1881, was originally designed for the Liverpool Philharmonic Society Theatre and how the cheaply printed Stations of the Cross were then being replaced with 'a set more worthy of the edifice'. The lower photograph, again to quote Mannex, shows the 'magnificent altar and reredos designed and carved by Neill & Pearson of Dublin'.

Mr and Mrs Oliver Chalker and family, c. 1924. The Salvation Army had practised Christianity in Barrow in a practical way since 1881. The endorsement on this photograph reads, 'Mr & Mrs Chalker and family who left Barrow for Norwich on Thursday May 29th 1924.' Their leaving must have been quite a loss for the Army in Barrow at the time. Mr Chalker, living in the Army's house at No. 50 Westgate Road, had been the Commandant at Barrow and the Army advertised during his time in charge – 'Band of Love, Monday 6.30, Young People's Legion, 7.30, Chums and Sunbeams, 6.30. Home League – women only – Mondays 3 p.m.' There were four Sunday services for adults and three for children and a public service nightly at 7.30 p.m. The Life Saving Girl Guards paraded on Mondays at 7 p.m. and the Life Saving Scouts on Tuesday at 7 p.m.

The Lads Red Triangle Club next to the Temperance Waverley Hotel in Abbey Road in the 1930s. This was the headquarters for the Young Men's Christian Association in Cumberland, Westmorland and Furness and advertised that 'splendid accommodation for leisure hours is afforded by reading, billiards and concert rooms. Premises open 1pm to 10pm. Membership fee six shillings – free for Army and Navy men.'

The 'international gymnastics team' of St Mark's, Barrow, in 1911. Revd F.W. Hopkins MA (Cantab) was the vicar, Revd L. Marner Smyth the curate, and Thomas Thompson the verger.

The Walney Ploughing Competition held at North Scale on 12 February 1912. 'The class of people who frequent these exhibitions is far from being their least interesting characteristic' said *The News* of 17 February 1912, ' – the great proportion of them are from the different branches of the agricultural pursuit.' The same verbose report continued, 'The meteorological conditions giving no sign of depression or rain the day's programme was gone through without a hitch.' Mr T. Dobson of Arnside, the first prize winner, is in the top picture. The lower picture shows Mr William Postlethwaite of Stank, followed closely by a judge, before being awarded second prize.

Two crowd scenes. At the top, the scene in Market Street, Barrow, on a busy market-day with the fair in the background, at the turn of the century. Below, the crowds assemble outside the Town Hall for Queen Victoria's Golden Jubilee celebrations in June 1887, when the Marquis of Hartington opened the new Town Hall and was presented with the freedom of the Borough. The marquis opened the building with a special gold key and there was a grand procession from the railway station.

An artist's impression of Empress Drive in the *Souvenir of Vickerstown* by J.C. Ferguson and L.A. Oates. Vickerstown, originally planned to be similar to Port Sunlight, was redesigned to be a 'marine garden city' but even that was never fully achieved. Empress Drive was built for the top management class of Vickers worker (see p. 101).

Mikasa Street (above) and Powerful Street (below), Vickerstown, which were designed as housing for the foremen and skilled workers. Some were 'even built with bathrooms'. 'The place is indeed quite of the model village lines,' said the Mannex guide, 'the number of inhabitants quickly increased from 474 in 1891 to over 6000 today [1910].'

Town End (above) and Mid Town (below), Biggar. Biggar is one of a number of ancient settlements which were absorbed by the Borough of Barrow as it expanded. Because of its location, however, Biggar remained isolated from development until the last few decades when a number of the old buildings were 'modernized'. When the pictures were taken the farmers in Biggar were William Parker Backhouse at No. 15 Biggar, Mrs Elizabeth Casson at South End, John Gilliland at Biggar, John Helm at Schoolhouse, Andrew and Isaac Riley at Nos 4 and 19 Biggar, Mrs Hannah Robinson at Town End and William Townson at No. 12 Biggar.

Artillery at camp at Walney at about the time of the First World War. Bulmer's guide of 1912 says, 'For the better protection of Barrow against foreign foes a new battery is in course of erection. It is intended for the Royal Garrison Artillery, two companies of which have been formed, organised and equipped since March 1910, and it is anticipated that, on the completion of the fort early in 1911, these companies will be well able to cope with the defense of the town.'

Trams decorated for the maiden run on the 'long talked of and quickly-laid tram route' to Biggar Bank on Walney, 'in time for the August Bank Holiday' on Friday 4 August 1911. Alderman J.P. Smith, chairman of the electricity committee of the Borough Council pointed, at the opening ceremony, to the cost of the undertaking at £7,000 and hoped it would soon become a paying concern. It was also said that in the course of five weeks the Highways Department had laid 13,000 square yards of macadam roadway. 'Within two months of the contract being signed the trams were running' said a report.

All the fun of the fair at Walney in the 1930s. Not quite Morecambe or Blackpool but a lot nearer to Barrow during those depressed years.

The 18th and 19th greens of the Barrow Golf Club in 1923. The club was founded in 1921 and the greens opened for play in June 1922. 'There is a commodious Clubhouse, well arranged with every convenience and service for the golfer' said the Furness Year Book. The captain was Dr J.A. Reed and the ladies' captain, Mrs W. Pass.

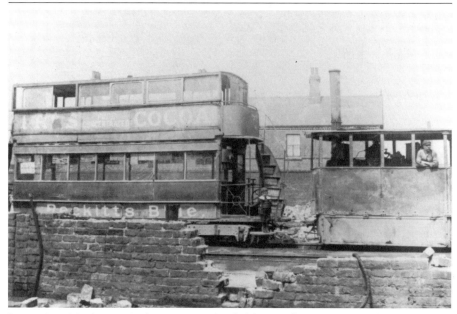

Barrow's original municipal trams were hauled by small steam-engines between 1885, when the steam trams started, and 1904, when the electrified system was introduced. The steam tram system had been opened on 11 July 1885 but the condition of the rolling stock had deteriorated by the time these pictures were taken at the turn of the century.

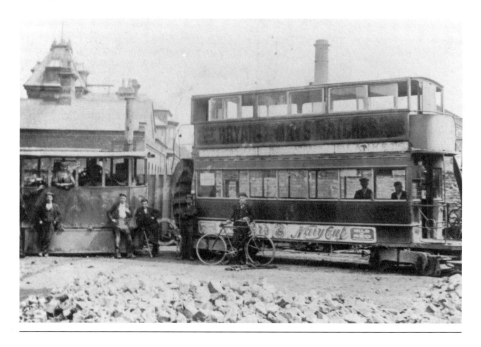

Abbey Road with stone sets and tramcar, *c.* 1905. The neatness and order of the street scene of those days contrasts with the untidy chaos of today. 'It is about 80 feet wide, with spacious footpaths, along which are planted sycamores and other quick-growing trees. Ornamental iron seats, the gift of various gentlemen of the town, have been placed at convenient distances; and when the trees have attained maturity Abbey Road will bear no remote resemblance to the celebrated boulevards of Paris,' said P. Mannex, who could not consider the effect of motor traffic.

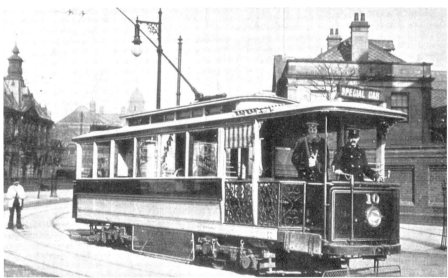

'The Roose Car' – tramcar No. 10 – in Ramsden Square, *c.* 1910. Note the elaborate wrought-iron railings and gate on the open platform where the driver and conductor are standing. The Roose cars had a lower roof because of the railway bridge in Salthouse Road.

The Biggar Bank tram, advertising the Coliseum Continous Pictures and Hutchinson Tyres, in the later years of the Barrow tramway. Motor buses were introduced in 1923 and the last tram ran in 1932. One can but wonder if they may return as society now tries to escape motor car pollution.

One of the fine single-deck tramcars used in Barrow, with more advertising this time for
E. Todd & Sons, Ladies and Gents Tailors. Note the style of the wrought-iron railings
and curtained windows.

The Farmers Arms at Old Newbarns, in the early years of this century. This was a typical nineteenth-century beerhouse and, at the time of the photograph, Jane Southwell was the landlady licensed to sell ale, beer, porter and tobacco. By 1912 the name over the door was Mrs Jane Fisher.

'The Oak Lea fire outrage' is the title of this photograph of 1913. Oak Lea at Sowerby Wood, Hawcoat, was built in 1874 for Henry William Schneider, the famous steelmaker entrepreneur, to the design of Paley & Austin of Lancaster. Schneider also had a mansion called Belsfield at Bowness on Windermere, but used Oak Lea for his many business visits to Barrow. It remained empty for many years after his death and rumours of its conversion into a sanatorium came to nothing. On 10 May 1913 fire started in suspicious circumstances, with many blaming the Suffragette movement, which was very active at the time. Oak Lea was destroyed and later demolished.

Pass & Co. of No. 100 Duke Street, Barrow. The company used this photograph to advertise their business. Betsy Pass advertised as toy, fancy goods, hosier and smallware dealer at this address in 1882, but by 1912 Pass & Co. were advertising from Nos 54 and 56 Duke Street. Ernest Pass, a son of this family, was killed in the First World War and his father, Alfred, of No. 17 Infield Park Road, gave the Barrow Cricket Club land off Abbey Road for their cricket ground as a memorial.

A. Hollis's Cavendish Studio, at No. 3 Cavendish Square opposite the Town Hall, at the turn of the century. Hollis advertised 'Royal photographer of 30 years experience.'

Gladstone Terrace above Greenbank, Hawcoat, c. 1912. The shop on the corner is a post office where Thomas Waite was subpostmaster, with collections at 7.45 a.m. and 6.30 p.m. on six days a week, and 7.45 a.m. on Sunday. William Woodburn Waite FSAA of Greenbank, Hawcoat, was the Barrow Borough Treasurer, George Barrow Waite of No. 8 Cliffe Lane, Hawcoat, was the Hawcoat quarry foreman, and George A. Waite of Summer Hill, Hawcoat, was the owner of G. & T. Waite's hay, straw and provender dealer business in Crellin Street. In 1884 Jane Waite was licensee at The Kings Arms, Hawcoat, and a Thomas Waite was the Hawcoat blacksmith.

Dalton Road near Abbey Road, at the turn of the century. Richard Coward Sykes's drapers shop is on the right with Richard Spencer's Dalton Road post office and stationers next door. The shop with the clock sign is that of W.T. Story, the watchmaker. On the left James Thompson, wine and spirit merchant, is next to Hugh Ledgerwood's grocery shop.

Inside the Barrow Steam Laundry in Hindpool Road about the time of the First World War. The proprietors were W. and A. Milligan, who lived at Hollingarth on Abbey Road. They advertised: 'Laundry work in all branches, dry cleaning and dyeing, suits spotted and pressed same day, curtain dressers, carpet beaters – the only way –, carpet cleaners – old like new –, glove cleaning – quick work. THE dry cleaners and dyers, mourning orders executed in 24 hours. Contractors to Hotels and County families. Parcels by rail or post. Quick despatch.'

The Dalton Road junction with Abbey Road. The top picture shows the Barrow Cooperative Society building on the right and on the opposite corner grocers and provision merchants the Cannon Brothers' Abbey Road Stores (they also had a shop at No. 84 Duke Street). The bottom view is of the impressive Barrow Cooperative Society Abbey Road building. The story of the early 'laboured beginnings' of the Barrow Cooperative movement after its founding in 1860 is to be found in Dr J.D. Marshall's *Furness and the Industrial Revolution*.

'Old Bill' at home and at the Front, on the Royalty Theatre float in the Barrow Peace celebrations parade, 19 July 1919. The festivities took place to celebrate the war to end all wars, twenty years before the start of the Second World War. The church bells were rung at intervals all day, and, after a victory march, there was a two minute silence at 12 noon. Tea was served in the afternoon for widows and parents of those who 'had fallen' and 'smoking concerts' were arranged in the evening at various locations for those who 'had served'.

Dunn's Clyno Charabanc, with daughter Mavis Dunn, the child near the front of the coach, in the late 1920s. Dunns of Barrow operated motor coaches from their garage in Duke Street. It was not unknown for Dunns to take the coach body off a chassis and mount a lorry body for a temporary period. (Ian Dunn of Crooklands has kindly loaned this and the pictures on pp. 134 and 135 from the family collection and provided the information on a previously unrecorded corner of Barrow history.)

Coronation celebrations in Barrow, 1911. The top picture shows the Rose Carnival with the Rose Queen and her attendants watching as the rosebuds dance, and in the lower picture the same troupe are seen in the parade through the town. 'The great feature of the day', said a report, 'was the schoolchildren's procession through the principal streets and subsequent Rose Carnival at Cavendish Park – a sight that will long be retained as a happy memory by all who witnessed it.'

The crowd at the Howe Street party during Peace Day celebrations, 19 July 1919. There were lots of flags and some people dressed up for the occasion. The Borough Council asked for no bonfires, fireworks or street decorations, Howe Street took no notice of the latter and had a party. Twenty-two years later the Second World War blitz was to ravage this street along with many others in the area. (Photo by Albert Turner of No. 18 Robert Street.)

A fairground crowd of mostly children at the turn of the century. All are dressed up for a day at the fair, with wide collars and Sunday best in many cases.

Sixteen-year-old Vera Wright, the Carnival Queen, 1936. Just before the war the annual carnival queen event was becoming nearly a 'beauty queen' festival in a way it had not been in earlier years. There were five finalists before the selection committee at the Town Hall on Thursday 14 May 1936 – Constance Trotter, Ena Timmings, Irene May Austin, Rosealeen Byers (all aged 18 years) and the eventual winner, Vera Wright.

Audrey Leitch, the Barrow Carnival Queen in 1939. The retiring queen, Miss Kathleen Reach, 'made a dignified entrance' at the Holker Street ceremony, and took her place on the throne to make a speech in which she thanked everyone for the splendid support given to the hospital. 'Then divesting herself of crown and sceptre she took her position at the side of the throne and the queen elect, Miss Audrey Leitch, supported by the ladies-in-waiting, Misses Doris Large and Betty Dickinson, made their entry to the applause of the crowd. Although the sun did not manage to grace the proceedings, the rain fortunately managed to hold off,' reported *The News* of Saturday 24 June 1939. The Second World War was only ten weeks away.

The hospital parade, 1938. Held just before the war the parade demonstrated the style of things to come – tin hats, gas masks and throw your pennies through Adolf's mouth. Men and women were training for the suffering to be inflicted on the town (see p. 82).

A dug-out bomb shelter in Barrow Park, photographed by T. Milligan of Kendal Street on 3 January 1940. The first winter of the war was a bad one (see p. 158).

Hall Street after the blitz, May 1941. The German bombers seeking Vickers caused extensive property damage to 'civilian housing'. Ninety-two people are reported to have been killed during the blitz, and 618 houses destroyed.

The Abbey Road Baptist chapel in April 1941 (see p. 94). One of the authors, as a nine-year-old, was taken by his great uncle and aunt, who lived in Hollow Lane and whose home was 'just missed' by the bombing, through streets of rubble the day after a raid to view the Abbey Road bomb damage.

Barrow Island street party to celebrate the end of the Second World War, 1945. The sense of community and of relief expressed in celebrations such as this were a joy for those lucky enough to take part.

Wilf Spencer before his benefit match of 1925. The Barrow Rugby Club dates back to 1876 and had grounds at Cavendish Park until 1914 and then at Little Park, Roose, until 1931 when the field was lost to housing. The badge on Wilf Spencer's chest is of the Northern Rugby Union.

The Barrow Association Football Club, winners of the Lancashire Combination championship for 1920/1. The club was founded in 1901 and reached a zenith as they joined the Third Division (Northern) of the national leagues in 1921.

The Rugby Football Club cup-tie team of 1922/3. Players were Burgess, Newman, Smith, Barnes, Jannicks, Brown, Carr, Sayle, W. Scott, E. Thornborrow, W. Spencer, J. Wallace, J. Hickman, W. Job. Their ground was Little Park, Roose. It would be eight years before the team would play at Craven Park.

H. Gifford in his Northern Rugby Union jersey and badge and wearing his 1906/7 cap. 'Cosma', in *The News* of 25 April 1908, wrote various reports on the Northern Union football season 1907/8: 'Gifford has been the most successful goal kicker for he has steered the ball between the posts on 16 occasions'; 'Gifford and Hannah have scored seven tries each'; 'Without a doubt Gifford has been the most prominent member of the team, his form having been brilliant all through the season . . . Gifford, Hannah and Kit Brown have also got County Honours and there was great disappointment in Furness when Gifford was overlooked for International honours.' We must wonder about the rest of the team when the report continues: 'Since the big cup-tie with Hunslett only one game has been won and that with the wooden spoonists'; 'So far as the position in the tables is concerned Barrow figures 14th on the list whilst last season they were 11th'; 'So far as the Lancashire Cup is concerned Barrow received the order of the knock in the first round being beaten at Oldham by 22 points to 3.'

FRANCO BRITISH EXHIBITION
LONDON 1908.

Stand 829 at the Franco-British exhibition in London, 1908. The Furness Railway decided to publicize their activities centred on Barrow when they displayed at the exhibition, although stand 829 was really the end of an era for them as Mr F.J. Ramsden, the superintendent, retired on the 31 July 1908. (He was presented with an Angelus piano by the Duke of Devonshire and fellow directors.) He was replaced by Mr Haynes. The opening of the exhibition on 14 May 1908 was the first in a series of noteworthy events that year. On 26 May the King and Queen and President Falliers of France visited the exhibition. On 7 August a mare and foal were killed on the line at Haverthwaite. On 12 August the 9.04 a.m. train was involved in an accident at Ulverston. On 13 August a gas balloon at the exhibition exploded killing two people. On 15 August 5,000 French people on a one-day trip visited the exhibition. On 5 September a man was found shot dead in a first class compartment of a Barrow to Carnforth train. On 10 September Mr Tyson, the station-master at Stainton, shot himself and his wife killed herself the following week. On 14 September Mr Cully, the Barrow station-master, was badly injured in a motor accident in Ramsden Square. On 19 October there was a robbery at the exhibition and £1,200 of precious metals was stolen. Hardly an uneventful exhibition time.

SECTION FOUR

Dalton and Surrounding Villages

The nave of Furness Abbey. Used in 1906 as a holiday postcard, the message reads, 'I went over to Fleetwood last night for the sail. It was lovely.'

The guide at Furness Abbey with four schoolgirls on the sedilia, 1905. The photograph carries the legend 'Our school journey to Furness Abbey 1905'. Bulmer's guide of the time begins, 'Where the setting sunbeams once gilded the deep-dyed windows rich with the figures of saints and warriors and all the emblazoned pomp of heraldry, now waves the monumental ivy with solemn motion as it keeps time to the sobbing wind that moans mournfully among the ruins. The deep mellow voices of the monks who here chanted the holy vespers have died away.' And so the description continues.

A group visiting Furness Abbey in winter during the 1920s. The entrance for visitors was by a small lodge on the hillside on the right of the photograph.

Furness Abbey station on the Furness Railway. This neat station was no doubt a show place being built near to the residence of Sir James Ramsden, general manager of the FR. The first printed pictures of this area were of Furness Abbey published in 1727, on the 600th anniversary of its foundation.

The Furness Abbey Hotel, when Frank C. Bright was manager, *c.* 1910. Bulmer's guide advised, 'it is a large and well appointed hostelry much frequented by tourists and visitors'. The lower picture shows the interior of the verandah. Note the FR advertising boards on the wall.

East View, Rampside, the home of John Pennington, *c.* 1910.

Rampside dwellings, *c.* 1910. The vicar at the time was Revd Samuel Atkinson Adams BA, and Miss M.A. Gibson was headmistress of the council school. Mrs Ryan occupied Beach Mount on the left of the upper photograph and Mr F. Griffen was at Cliffe House on the other side of the road. Waver, pictured below, was occupied by the Pearsons.

The dismantling of Stank mine buildings, probably in the 1920s. The mine buildings had lasted many years after the mine closed but when the Ulverston to Barrow coast road was built the stone of the buildings was used as hard core. The Dunn family owned the mine buildings on their land at Stank, and George Dunn is seen with his workmen and flat-backed lorry opposite, while a building is demolished by explosives above and below.

Dendron church and its interior, *c.* 1904. On 3 December of that year the vicar, Revd Arthur James Humphris, was found shot, not fatally, in his bedroom. The picture below shows the church's fine collection of oil lamps. A chapel was built in the village, which is mentioned in Domesday Book, in 1642 by Robert Dickinson for divine worship on Sunday and to serve as a school on weekdays. It was replaced by the church in 1776, which itself was enlarged in 1795.

Bousfield Farm, Stank, farmed in 1910 by Robert Hilton Edmondson. The hole visible in the lower picture was due to iron mining subsidence and has since been filled in. The Stank mine closed in 1901 (see also pp. 134 and 135).

Gleaston Ploughing Competition, *c.* 1910. Success depended principally upon the contestant's ability to produce a straight line.

The village of Gleaston, with the police station and notice-board on the left, *c.* 1905. Note the pre-Macadam road surface.

Gleaston mill, *c.* 1907, and mill-house, *c.* 1912. In 1907 the mill was occupied by Thomas Huartson. It has been recently restored. Gleaston, referred to as Glassertun in Domesday Book, is now a popular dormitory village.

The village post office, part of Mrs Margaret Thompson's grocers shop at Crown Cottage, Scales. Scales is a small hamlet in the parish of Aldingham. The name is of Norse origin, 'skali' meaning 'hut'.

The Salvation Army marches along Broughton Road, Dalton-in-Furness, on Good Friday 1931. The officers at Dalton were then Capt. Sydney Bishop and Lieut. George Milburn.

Dalton Cricket Club, resplendent in their ringworm caps and whites, and with their terrier mascot, in 1913. The umpire's cap seems capable of holding a much larger head than the one in it. The club secretary was George Denny.

Miss Elsa Jackson, the Dalton Parade Queen, 28 June 1924. Elsa was the daughter of the licensee of the Lord Nelson Hotel. *The News* described her dress as 'of white satin trimmed with pearls and diamonds panelled with lace . . . her chaplet was of silver leaves and pink roses, her bouquet was of Merechal Niel roses presented by her grandmother. A chill wind was blowing bearing a few drops of cold rain. The Queen very gracefully played her part bowing to the repeated plaudits of the crowd.'

Two imposing Dalton buildings, Dowdales mansion (above) and the police station (below, *c*. 1904). The mansion became a Central Selective School in 1928 and has been much developed since that time. The Lancashire Constabulary police station is reported in James E. Walton's *History of Dalton-in-Furness* as having 'opened in 1897 and continued in use until 1968'.

The Market Cross with South Kellgate, the road out to Askam, *c.* 1902. Off the picture to the left is Dalton Castle, a mid-fourteenth-century pele tower built for protection against the marauding Scots.

Market Street, Dalton, at the turn of the century. Of interest is the 'tar-spray' experimental road surface work shown by the dark patches.

The Clarence Hotel, Ulverston Road, Dalton, in 1900. The proprieter at the time was J.T. Slater, who advertised 'the large club room and good accommodation for cyclists and footballers'.

Upper Market Street with Tudor Square in the background. The shop of the photographer, Thomas Charles Hoskins, printer, stationer, music and book seller, is on the left, while at the end of the street, on the right, is The Black Bull, whose landlord at the time was John Benson. The police station stands opposite, manned by Inspector Richard Hume, Sergeants Lawrence Moore and Ellis Raymond Edge and Constables Murray, Parker and Potts.

Dalton parish church presides over Goose Green, Dalton. On the way to Furness Abbey, the workhouse and the National School were situated at Goose Green, with the gasworks close by.

A garden party in Dalton, *c.* 1905. The message on the postcard, posted on 24 August 1905 to Mrs Atkinson of Castle View, Dalton, reads 'What do you think of this? I thought you would like one as you have come out so well. It might have been taken for our benefit. Love, Lizzie.'

The Dalton main street near the Wellington Hotel on a parade day, *c.* 1910. The standard bearer next to the Chairman of the UDC is advertising a collection for widows and orphans. Three small men in the front row of the band seem quite overpowered by their tubas, and straw hats are the order of the day. The Dalton Prize Band conductor was John Henry Carter, music teacher, of No. 10 Market Street.

A group of Dalton schoolchildren, *c*. 1920. The children carry flags, fans and fancy wreaths for what was possibly an Empire Day celebration.

High Cocken, Barrow, *c*. 1920. This was once the home of the artist George Romney, 1742–55. It was extended in the early twentieth century by the Furness Railway Company and featured as a tourist attraction – but not on this photograph, which shows a near ruin.

A rare view from early this century of the old Furness Railway station at Lindal, now demolished, with its traditional part sandstone buildings. The Dalton–Lindal railway extension was completed in 1851 to cope with the iron ore traffic. This increased and in 1859 an iron works was built at Barrow – the forerunner of the Barrow Haematite Steel Company.

The legendary Lindal Moor Cricket Club pavilion earlier this century. The club celebrated its centenary with a programme of events in 1984. The peak of its performance was in 1977 when they reached the final of the Haig Village Cricket Championship at Lords against Cookley. They unfortunately lost by twenty-eight runs, but the enthusiasm spread over the whole Furness area.

Lowfield pit, Lindal, in full production with Furness Railway wagons in front of the mine shaft, c. 1910. The pit was sunk to 500 ft below sea level to obtain iron ore. The main Furness rail line ran conveniently past the site. A common feature of the time was to issue a picture postcard on the death of a member of the pit staff. The proceeds of the sale of the card would go to the family.

Miners at Dickie Pink's iron mine at Newton-in-Furness between the wars. There are smiles on the faces of some of the miners, although the years of toil can also be seen. The mine was in use from 1903–44.

The Furness and District Bowling League committee in 1929. The Dalton CC Bowling Section secretary at the time was W. Mason of No. 22 Cleator Street.

The end view of one blast furnace and the disproportionate chimney of Askam iron works at the turn of the century, with Black Combe shadowy in the background. The iron works closed during the depression of the 1920s.

DALTON ROAD, ASKAM.

Two street scenes in Askam, *c.* 1908. The above shows Dalton Road facing the Furness Railway line, on the right. Occupants of the road at the time included William Charles Walker, miner and property owner, at No. 31 and William Longstaff, the joiner, at No. 13. The lower picture shows the junction of Duke Street and Duddon Road, where William Stelfox Jervis ran his grocers shop in 1910.

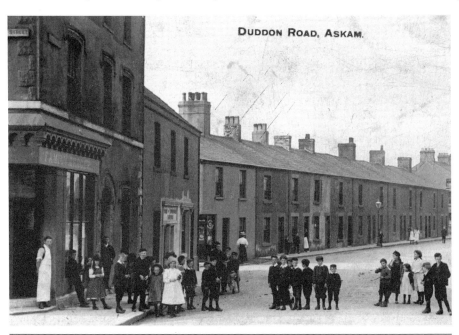

DUDDON ROAD, ASKAM.

Askam station on the Furness Railway, *c.* 1910. The road continues over the crossing in a straight line from Ireleth to the iron-red sand dunes of the Duddon estuary, from which you could once see the flames of the Millom iron works. (Both this card and the one below were published by Miss Margaret Bradshaw Cook of the post office and stationers at No. 13 Duke Street, Askam.)

Ireleth mill with part of the steeply sloping beck diverted along a race to the overshot wheel, on a card posted in 1906. The miller, covered in flour, is standing by the door.

Ireleth village, with the Traveller's Rest on the right, *c.* 1910. Jane Massicks was licensee. Mrs Margaret Parker ran the sub-post office.

A village band, possibly Askam, followed by the Boys Brigade, wends its way up the steep hill to Ireleth church for the Sunday school flower service in 1906. Askam and the Duddon estuary can be seen in the distance. The Askam Prize Band secretary was Thomas Satterthwaite. The Ireleth church vicar was the Revd T.A. Leonard and the curate the Revd G. Clayton.

Snow scenes in 1940. The picture above shows the Kirkby road at Askam. The group clearing the road includes William Robertson, Bobby Vickers, Bobby Robinson, W. Brown, M. Todd with, on the far left, Betty Moore from the post office. The lower picture shows the huge snow drift on Ireleth hill. During this hard winter, funerals were conducted on horse-drawn sledges and food was in short supply in Askam due to the rail line being blocked. Cinema-goers travelling from Askam to Dalton walked over a snow-covered double-decker bus on a hill near to Greenscoe quarries.

A cart prepared for the Dalton parade around the time of the First World War. The cart illustrates the combination of rural and industrial life in the Barrow area and completes our journey through the district.

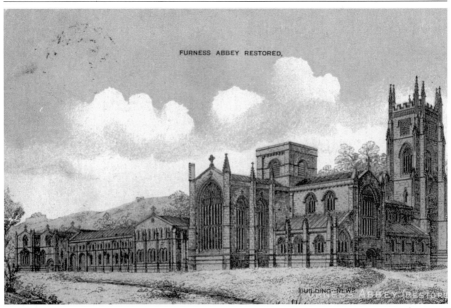

FURNESS ABBEY RESTORED,

An artist's impression of a reconstructed Furness Abbey. The illustration appeared in *Building News* at the turn of the century and caught the imagination of many.

Acknowledgements

The production of this book would not have been possible without the special assistance, in various ways, of the following people:

Barbara Garbutt and Jean Marsh • Mr Neil Honeyman • Mr George Dawson
Mr Leslie Marsh • Mr Ian Dunn

and the good people of Barrow and District, into whose lives and families this book intrudes, and those who encourage us in various ways in our collection of local photographic images.